М.

Learn how to Meditate the Easy way in 24 Hours: The Most Practical, Complete and Modern Guide on Meditation

Meditation

Learn how to Meditate the Easy way in 24 Hours

The Most Practical, Complete and Modern Guide on Meditation

By: Robert Junior

© Copyright 2015 Robert Junior

Preface

First of all, let me tell you that you really need to be very happy for downloading my book: ***"Meditation"***.

This book is in a nutshell the most complete, practical and modern guide a person can read today on meditation. It contains all the steps necessary beautifully combined with lots of pictures and illustrations in order to get you started on the wonderful world of meditation. As you are going to find out by reading this book, through the practice of meditation, you will be able to lower your stress levels, lose weight, become fitter and improve the overall level of your living conditions.

Throughout this book I am going to analyze in great detail many tips and tricks you can use in order not only to get in control of the whole thing but stay in control for the years to come.

As long as you follow the steps and guidelines you will read in this book I can guarantee you that you are going to see the first actual results and feel the difference within weeks.

This book will provide a lot of details on what is meditation, why is it important to practice it, how to be a meditation practitioner, in what aspects of your life you are going to see major improvement and how to stay on track in order to achieve your goals as fast as possible.

Thanks again for downloading this book, I hope you enjoy it!

Table Of Contents

Preface 4

Table Of Contents 5

Introduction – History to Meditation........................... 7

Chapter One – The Benefits of Meditation 9

Chapter Two – The Basics of Meditation.................... 12

Chapter Three – Main Types of Meditation............... 17

Chapter Four – Concentrative Meditation and Practices 23

Chapter Five – Open Awareness Meditation and Practices .32

Chapter Six – Mindfulness and Practices 44

Chapter Seven - Guided Meditation and Practices.............52

Chapter Eight – Mixed Meditation Practices............................54

Conclusion 59

Free Book.. 70

Introduction – History to Meditation

There are techniques of Buddhism, such as meditation, that anyone can adopt.

~ Dalai Lama

Meditation is an ancient practice that is believed to have originated from the Indus Valley. This is where archeologists found wall art that dated back to 3,500 BC depicting people who sat in postures that we would recognize today as meditation postures. Indian scriptures that date back 3,000 years also describe meditation techniques.

Throughout the years after meditation was discovered, religions across the globe adopted various techniques and practices that mimicked meditation. Meditation was introduced to the United States at the same time Yoga was introduced in the early 20th century, and in the '60's there was an explosion of interest in the practice.

Judaism has Hitbodedut and Islam has Tafakkur as well as Sufism. Buddhism uses numerous different forms of meditation, although that's not shocking considering meditation evolved in the Indian region. Even Christianity practices meditation, especially the monks. Monks spend hours inside a room contemplating God daily, which is a form of quiet meditation. Even Catholics use meditation by counting their rosary beads.

So, as you can see, meditation is a worldwide accepted practice of quieting the mind as well as the soul. However, you don't have to be religious in order to believe in and practice the art of meditation. It's simply a tool that will help you relieve your daily stress and help you know yourself better.

Each type of meditation has its unique aspects and should be explored by a person who would like to learn about meditation. You never know if one technique will be better than the other for you if you don't try them. So I encourage you to try out each type a few times before you switch to the next in order to see if it will help you feel calmer and relaxed.

First, let's take a look at the benefits of meditation.

Chapter One – The Benefits of Meditation

Meditation is the practice of achieving a quiet state of mind. There are several different ways to achieve this, which will be discussed in Chapter Two. The more common technique is a sitting position with the legs crossed Lotus style and the hands on the knees. However, there are various different styles and techniques used in meditation such as walking, standing, slow movements, and sitting. For beginners, twenty minutes of meditation daily will help you get into the habit of meditating and help you understand the practice. You can gradually add time to your meditation as you feel more comfortable with it.

So why should you be meditating?

For starters, it's free. Meditation is something you can do anywhere and you can easily practice this on your own with a few guided techniques. It's been proven to be a great short-term stress reliever and a long-term health benefit to those who practice, and the benefits can be felt immediately. However, meditation does take practice and patience.

Compared to other stress-reduction exercises, meditation is one of the better choices because there are no side effects from herbal remedies or prescribed medications. In addition, it's excellent for those who are not able to do strenuous exercises, but it still has some of the benefits of exercise. And the meditation helps us free ourselves from the daily stresses of life without thinking about them.

The first and most prominent benefit to meditation is relaxation. When you are focusing, whether it's on many objects, one object, or on nothing, your mind delves into the theta wave range, which is where your mind is free to think and form thoughts without fear of guilt or shame. In this state, you're more likely to form ideas that are out of the box and your body is more relaxed. Sometimes, people reach this state of mind while they're driving on the highway and can't remember the last five minutes, or while they is brushing their hair in the morning.

Some other psychological benefits to meditation are:

- A boost in happiness by increasing positive emotions, decreasing depression, decreasing anxiety, and decreasing stress.
- Gives you a boost in self-control by helping you regulate emotions and allows you to introspect.
- Improves your productivity by increasing your focus, attention, and ability to multi-task, memory, and ability to be creative.

Meditation is also great for your health. The most common referenced physical benefit is the reduction of stress levels, which affect your health immensely. In fact, most diseases and illnesses that we know of today are actually a secondary illness to stress. Therefore, by reducing your stress levels, you will live a much healthier, vibrant life.

Some other physical benefits of meditation include:

- An increased immune system function.
- Decreased sensitivity to pain.
- Decreased inflammation on the cellular levels.
- Increases the gray matter in your brain.

- Increases the volume of your brain in sections that relate to emotional regulation, positive emotions, and self-control.
- Increases thickness in areas that correspond with focus.
- Lowers your blood pressure while you're meditating and for hours afterward.
- Improves blood flow and circulation throughout your body.
- Lowers your heart rate and respiratory rate.
- Lower your cortisol levels and gives you a feeling of deep relaxation and well-being.

So, as you can see, meditation is an excellent way to make yourself a healthier, happier, better-rounded individual. Remember that you do not have to believe in any type of higher power or being in order to practice meditation, but you can incorporate that into your sessions if you are religious. Either way, meditation is an excellent way to reduce stress levels in your life and get you started on a path to enlightenment and understanding.

Chapter Two – The Basics of Meditation

While there are hundreds of different ways to meditate, they all have a few things in common. This chapter is designed to help you figure out where you should be meditating and what state of mind you should be in when you begin. You'll learn how to sit if your meditation involves sitting, and how to relax your spine while keeping your back straight, and much more.

Where to Meditate

Ultimately, you should choose a place that makes you feel comfortable and at peace, and it should be free of distractions. However, sometimes this isn't feasible and you must learn to quiet your mind while you're in the midst of a crowd or riding on the subway, but that takes practice. When you first start, try to find a quiet place.

In addition to a quiet place, make sure it's comfortable! You don't want to be in a room that is too hot and will make you fall asleep. In the same moment, you don't want to be somewhere too cold or you'll just keep thinking about how cold you are. Choose a comfortably heated or cooled room that you won't feel hot or cold in.

Where you choose to meditate based on whether or not you're sitting, standing or moving is also imperative. If you're sitting, you want to be sure that you're in a comfortable position and you're not going to fall asleep. So sitting in a chair or on the floor with a cushion beneath your bottom are both good options. Lying back on the couch is probably not a good idea. If you're standing, wear comfortable shoes and clothing, and make sure that you're not going to fall into anything. And if you're walking, be sure that you're also wearing comfortable shoes and that you're not going to walk into anything.

Your Posture

During meditation, your posture is very important because you don't want to end giving yourself health complications while you're trying to do something good for yourself. With a bad posture, you could end up damaging your spine, but you shouldn't have good posture just while you're meditating. Try to practice good posture no matter what you're doing.

In order to have good posture, you must learn how to relax while you're keeping your spine straight. Start by sitting with your spine straight with a natural curve in your lower back. Now pull back your shoulders gently but keep them relaxed. As you're moving your shoulders back, your chest should open and your chin should go up. You should feel comfortable and relaxed in this position. You'd be surprised by how long you can hold this position if you're doing it correctly!

When you're meditating, you should change your posture from time to time in order to invoke various mental energies. You can practice cross-legged meditation, walking meditation, yoga or even tai chi meditation where you're gently moving into different positions.

Meditation Mindset

You should be meditating when you feel calm. Therefore, you may need to do a few exercises or stretches before you meditate in order to get you into the correct mindset. Meditating while you're still thinking about all the stressful problems you had to deal with that day is not going to be easy, so beginners should be sure to do something else that eases them into a calm state before they start meditating.

You can take a walk, take a bath, or even do a little yoga before you start a concentration or mindfulness type meditation.

Focus on Your Breathing

It's important to not force your breathing patterns, but it should be slow and rhythmic. Focusing on the breathing is used in a lot of meditation techniques in order to focus the mind, but some meditation techniques actually recommend breathing to be in a natural pattern, whether that's quick or slow for the individual. Therefore, focusing on your breathing is dependent upon which type of meditation you are performing.

Don't Be Hungry

If you eat right before meditation, you may become sleepy and unable to focus. If you don't eat a little before meditation and you're hungry, you won't be able to focus. Basically, you should be sure that you eat normally and choose a meditation time where you won't be starving or you won't be trying to digest.

In addition to not being hungry, don't be thirsty. You should drink a little water before meditation, but not enough that you'll have to interrupt your meditation time in order to go to the bathroom.

Keep a Schedule

In order to create a habit, you have to do something every day for thirty days. Ideally, you should be doing meditation at the same time every day for the same amount of time in order for it to become something that you regularly do without thinking about it.

When you first start meditating, you might want to start out slow. Fifteen to thirty minutes a day is a good time to start with, and then go up in increments from there. However, some people who have been meditating for years still only do fifteen to thirty minutes of meditation daily. It's best to devote a small amount of time each day rather than to devote a few hours during a few days a week.

Be Patient

You're going to have a hard time shutting off your mind completely, so if you're attempting a meditation technique where this is supposed to happen, don't be frustrated if you don't achieve a quiet mind for quite some time. Meditation takes a lot of practice and discipline, and it can be difficult to achieve mindfulness when you're just beginning.

Practice Being Mindful

Even after you're done with a meditation session, your meditation is not over. This is a lifestyle, not just an exercise you do every day. Practice being mindful of every situation you're in because being in the present is the best part of life.

Imagine that you're sitting at a dinner table and everyone has their cell phones out. They're not listening to each other talk or engaging in interesting conversations because they're too busy spending time with someone who is not even present. Being mindful is being able to put away that cell phone and focus on the people and happenings around you.

Knowing the basics of meditation before you begin any of the practices mentioned later in this book will help you understand how to perform them better. Now, let's talk about the different types of meditation so that you can narrow down your choice of meditation technique further.

Chapter Three – Main Types of Meditation

There are so many different types of meditation, and all of them are unique in their own way. First, I'll talk about the four main types of meditation, and then I'll mention some other types that are not as well-known, but they're just as important. Some of these meditation techniques use silence while others use external and internal noises in order to focus the mind.

Concentrative Meditation

Most instructors actually start their students off with this type of meditation because it teaches us how to focus our minds. In this type of meditation, an object is used in order to focus the mind on a single-pointed attention such as a sound, image, flame, or breath. When just beginning, most people choose to use the breath as their focal point because it's very easy to monitor our breaths.

This technique is meant to teach the meditator how to develop the ability to stay calm, be grounded, and stabilize their thought-process. The most well-known concentrative meditation technique is Transcendental Meditation.

Open Awareness

This type of meditation is used to teach the mind to stay focused while there are distractions around. It's like looking at the world with a wide-angle camera lens and still being able to be aware of one's self and inner thoughts. Open awareness teaches us how to be aware of the present despite other things that might be happening around us.

A common technique that uses open awareness is Zen practices such as zazen or shikantaza. These are two popular forms that are practiced in Western culture.

Mindfulness

Mindfulness is the most popular and well known meditation technique. It is also the most researched by scientists. It's a combination of concentration and open awareness meditation techniques, and can be found in numerous contemplative traditions. It's commonly associated with the Buddhist practice of Vipassana or 'insight meditation.'

When practicing mindfulness, the practitioners focus on their breath, bodily sensations, thoughts, feelings or sounds, but it's not as narrow as a concentrative meditation technique. Mindfulness is often used during daily tasks such as eating, driving, housework, walking or jogging.

Guided Meditation

This is as it sounds. All types of meditation can be guided and are often practiced with others or a recording in order to get the mindset right. In one form of guided meditation, the meditator uses audio guidance from an instructor that brings about certain images, affirmations, states of mind, or imagined desired experiences. It's popular in the West as a way to bring about a sense of well-being and health. IT's often used before a surgery or an athletic performance in order to bring about a successful outcome to the event.

Now that you're aware of the four main types of meditation let's look at some of the sub-types of meditation. Even famous people you may know use a lot of these techniques around the world today. If you'd like, you can find different classes that will help you in guided meditation with these different types.

Primordial Sound Meditation

Used by Lady Gaga and Dr. Deepak Chopra, primordial sound meditation is silent and uses a mantra. This mantra is one that you receive from an instructor and is a vibrational sound that correlates with a sound of the universe that was happening at the time and place of your birth. The Vedic mathematic formula is used in order to create the sound for you.

This method of meditation is best practiced while you're sitting down in order to feel more relaxed and comfortable. It helps you enter into a deeper level of awareness because it takes you away from the intellectual side of your brain and brings you to the core of your mind.

Mindfulness-Based Stress Reduction

Jon Kabat-Zinn is the founder of this meditation technique. He created it in order to bring about a partnership in care between a patient and his or her medical team. Social workers, nurses, physicians, psychologists, and other health professionals in over two hundred medical centers around the world often use it.

Mindfulness-based stress reduction uses body scan and breath awareness in order to calm the mind. The patient focuses on their breath as they inhale and exhale and they focus attention on body parts. They start with the toes and work their way up to the top of their head. The person meditating can be sitting, standing or walking based upon the technique they're using.

Zen

Zen or Zazen translates to 'seated meditation'. It's origins come from Buddhism, but it's more of a philosophy than a religion. Zen uses the breath as a focal point and often there is an instructor that will help the students relax and stay centered on their thoughts.

This practice emphasizes enlightenment and focuses on the Sutras, doctrine taught through interaction with an instructor. There may be chanting involved with some of these meditation techniques.

Transcendental Meditation

A form of concentrative meditation, transcendental meditation uses a mantra, usually consisting of Sanskrit words, in order to help the practitioner focus. The mantra is determined by the student's birth date, gender, and the year the instructor was trained. This is a seated meditation that was made famous by the Beetles.

Kundalini Yoga

Working with an instructor is a large part of this tradition because there are hundreds of different hand positions depending upon the student's goal, whether it is stress relief, relief from addictions or increased vitality.

Kundalini yoga uses breath, mantras, mudras and focus. It was created by Yogi Bhajan.

Movement Meditation Techniques

Some meditation techniques require that the person actively move. You may engage in a repetitive activity that helps you achieve mindfulness or a concentrative state, and it helps you experience flow as you meditate.

Famous movement meditation techniques include walking meditation, yoga, and even gardening.

Spiritual Meditation

While most meditation techniques do not require that you believe in a higher being or powers within the universe, there are some that allow for spirituality to be inserted into the practice. For example, some mindfulness meditation techniques use prayers in order to focus the mind and heal the body. Meditation itself can be a spiritual practice that doesn't focus on any one religion, yet it does acknowledge that there is some sort of higher power or universe powers.

Some spiritual meditation requires the practitioner to focus on a singular question in order to get an answer from a higher being, while others require that the practitioner clear their mind completely and accept whatever may come their way that day.

As you can see, there are meditation techniques that use sounds, sights, smells, tastes, and touch in order to focus the mind, and there are others that refrain from using any of these senses. You have to choose which meditation technique is best for you.

In the next chapter, we'll talk about some of the more famous concentrative meditation techniques.

Chapter Four – Concentrative Meditation and Practices

Remember that concentrative meditation is using a focal point in order to bring about inner peace of the mind and quietness to the soul. Concentrative meditation can focus on the breath, a candle flame, or any other object. It's thought to first be discovered by the prehistoric man by gazing into the flames of his campfire for hours.

Basic Concentrative Meditation

This is a common form used to teach beginners how to quiet their minds and focus fully on their breaths. Make sure that you are in a sitting position on a chair with a straight spine and you are away from the back of your chair. Be sure that your feet are flat on the floor and your arms are straight. Now, turn your palms upward at your hips and relax your body.

In order to relax your body to prime you for meditation, try these steps.

- Inhale quickly through your nose with one short inhalation and one long inhalation.
- Then tense your body until your vibrating.
- Now hold your breath and the tension in your body for five seconds.

- Exhale forcibly through your mouth with one short exhalation and one long exhalation, the opposite of your inhalations.
- Throw the tension from your body as you exhale.
- Repeat these steps several times in order to get your body relaxed and your mind in a state of calmness and focus.

Once you've mastered this, you can move on to the actual technique.

- Inhale very slowly as you count to eight.
- Hold your breath for eight seconds.
- Exhale slowly for eight seconds.
- Do not pause between an exhale and an inhale. Simply inhale again without a pause and hold, and then exhale for a count of eight.

You can repeat this exercise three to six times and then take a break. You'll be surprised by how centered and loose you feel after this exercise. Your mind will feel lighter and you'll wonder why you were stressed in the first place.

If you have problems breathing, you can vary the counting times, but always keep them even. For example, you can inhale for three seconds, hold for three seconds, and exhale for three seconds.

Hong-Sau Technique of Concentration

Before we get started, Hong rhymes with song and Sau rhymes with saw. That way you're not confused about what you should be saying during this technique. As you've probably already gathered, the Hong-Sau method uses a nonverbal mantra in order to bring about a concentrative state. The words are actually an ancient Sanskrit mantra that means 'I am He' or 'I am Spirit'. This method does not control the breath but simply observes it.

You can practice this method either sitting down or standing up.

- Allow your next breath to come in on its own accord and as it does, mentally say the word Hong.
- Exhale naturally and mentally say the word Sau.
- Do not attempt to control your breathing as you do so.

You may notice the breaths first in your diaphragm and then in your lungs, but try to feel it in your nostrils and sinuses. This practice is all about being aware of the breaths and the body, but not controlling it.

- Once you're comfortable with the breathing, move on to the eye movements.
- Close your eyes and turn your gaze upward toward your third eye or the point between your eyebrows.
- Try to feel the flow of breath closest to your spiritual eye and focus on it.
- Do not allow the eyes to follow the movement of the breath as you're breathing.
- If you start to wander in your mind, calmly bring yourself back to what you're doing.
- Finish off by inhaling through the nose once, and then exhale three times through the mouth.

Enjoy the Stillness

In order to practice this technique you should be enjoying the stillness. Forget about your breaths and concentrate your focus at the center point between your eyebrows. Continue this for at least five minutes and you can choose to finish up with a prayer or just acknowledge the peacefulness you're feeling.

Ways to Deepen Your Meditation

Once you're comfortable with this form of meditation and you have the basics under control, you can try to deepen your meditation technique using these methods.

1. Relax the Body

New meditators often tense their body in an effort to concentrate, which is counterproductive. Deep concentration is only achieved when you are in a state of complete relaxation. Therefore, you should practice the tense and relax technique mentioned earlier in this chapter. This will help you feel looser and ready to meditate.

2. Pray

If you're religious, you can bring prayer into your meditation or you can do this before or after in order to make yourself feel more centered and connected to your higher being of choice.

3. Sit Perfectly Still

When you move your body, you are sending energy to your muscles rather than to your brain. The entire purpose of meditation is to send all of that energy into your mind in order to achieve your desired results. Therefore, you must sit still while you are meditating.

Doing some visualization for the first five minutes before you meditate is a good way to get your body to stop fidgeting. Try to think of yourself as a rock, solid and unmovable. Your body will grow calm on its own accord if you truly believe that you are as solid and unmovable as a rock.

Your physical restlessness will disappear if you sit still for long enough.

4. Eye Position

When you're practicing this technique your eyes should be closed and held steady as you look upwards as if you're looking at something an arm's length away and level with your head. Keep your gaze gently raised during your practice as this will bring the energy from the rest of your body to the highest spinal center, the third eye.

5. Do Not Control Your Breath

It seems a little odd, but in this meditation exercise, it is imperative that you do not control your breath. After your beginning breathing exercises, the controlling of your breath should cease. Let your breaths flow naturally and don't be alarmed by any pauses during or in-between your inhalations and exhalations as this is normal.

Enjoy the pauses in your inhalations and exhalations, as these are a sign of a deep state of advanced meditation and means that you are making excellent progress! Sometimes, your breathing may become so shallow and the pause so prolonged that you may feel it's hardly necessary to breathe at all. Don't be alarm by this as it's a natural process of deep meditation.

Tratak

Image courtesy of SOMMAI at FreeDigitalPhotos.net

Tratak is a form of concentrative meditation that is deeply rooted in our ancestor's practices of meditation. It uses a candle flame or fire in order to achieve deep meditation, and is an excellent way to rid your mind of distractive thoughts.

Tratak is beneficial for attention focus and memory enhancement.

- Practice a deep breathing exercise before you begin.
- Light ghee lamp or candle wherever you are comfortable and sit straight in a chair with good posture or on the floor cross-legged. If you're more advanced, you can sit in the Full Lotus Pose.
- Keep the flame twelve to twenty-four inches away from your face and be sure that it's at eye level, so place it on

top of a stack of books or on a tabletop. Just be sure it won't topple over!

- Now, take a few deep breaths and then gaze at the flame without blinking for as long as you can. Don't be alarmed if tears start to develop in your eyes. Keep your eyes focused and gaze at the flame only, nothing else around it.
- If thoughts develop, acknowledge them and simply let them go.
- Once your tears start to flow, close your eyes and keep your eyes closed as you see the imprint of the flame upon the inside of your eyelids.
- Bring your attention to your third eye and allow a feeling of peace to permeate your body.
- Once the flame has diminished from your internal sight, slowly open your eyes but do not look at the flame.
- It is recommended that you look at some sort of greenery or living plant for a few moments because Tratak increases the heat energy in your eyes. Use a drop of rosewater or another eye drop in order to refresh your eyes.

It will take time for your pineal function to be restored to its peak as you practice this method. Only look at the flame once and then put everything away until the next day. It's best to do this practice at either sunrise or sunset in order to get the best results. When you do start to experience results, you will have enhanced brave wave functions and a deeper knowledge of yourself.

Japa

Japa uses visualization in order to concentrate your mind to one focus. Thoughts may arise as you're practicing this method, but just let them float away. You may choose to use the sounds between the letters or you may choose to be silent, but know that the sounds help you focus better.

- Close your eyes and envision the letter A. See it in your mind's eye and picture as clearly as you can. Keep this in your field of vision for a moment.
- Then visualize the letter B just to the right of the letter A. See it as clearly as you possibly can and view it as a solid. Keep that in your field of vision for a moment.
- Now shift your focus to the space in between the two letters A and B and do Japa. This is making the sound 'Ahh' as you focus on that empty space between the two letters.
- Continue the sound for at least ten second and focus on that sound as much as you can. Feel the sound vibrating in your throat and how it enters the room. Keep your focus on the sound of 'Ahh' and try not to let your mind wander. Firmly bring it back to what you are doing if it starts to.
- Make this sound twice while you're focusing on the space between the two letters. Then focus on the sound 'Ahh' only.
- Now focus on the letter B and see that letter in your mind's eye. Picture just as you picture the letter A and keep in your focus for a moment.
- Visualize the next letter, C, and place it just to the right of the letter B.
- Now shift to the space in between the two letters and make the sound 'Ahh' again.

- Make the sound twice as you focus on the space between the letters. Continue with this method until you reach the letter G.

Once you reach the letter G, you can stop meditating or you can choose to continue on if you have not reached a feeling of inner peace and harmony.

These four methods can all be used by beginners and experienced meditators. Remember that these are concentrative methods and your thought process should be focused on the meditation rather than any stray mental comments you may have. Always acknowledge your thoughts and then visualize them leaving you as you concentrate on your meditation again.

Now, let's look at some open awareness meditation practices in Chapter Five.

Chapter Five – Open Awareness Meditation and Practices

Open-awareness meditation is like a wide angle lens. It takes in everything at once, including what is happening inside and outside of the body. You do not focus on any particular object during this practice, but rather focus on everything that comes into your mind's eye. It's often compared to the mind being like the open sky and the thoughts are clouds passing by. The practitioner acknowledges these thoughts and allows them to float by.

Popular methods include Zen zazen and shikantaza meditation.

Zen Zazen

Zen zazen focuses on every part of the body and the senses. In other meditation techniques, they tend to see the body, breath, and mind as separate entities, but Zen zazen sees them all as coming together as one. The first thing you need to pay attention to in Zen zazen is the position of the body.

Body Position

The position of your body communicates both outwardly and inwardly with your surroundings, and it has a lot to do with how your mind is acting and your breathing. There are numerous different body positions in Zen zazen, but the best one to use is the seated Buddha. Use a zafu or a small pillow to raise your behind off the floor and make things more comfortable. Your knees should be able to touch the ground comfortably. You should be sitting cross-legged.

There are various different styles of sitting cross-legged with a zafu beneath you.

When you are in the full-lotus position, the one commonly used by experienced practitioners, you should look something like this:

Image courtesy of tungphoto at FreeDigitalPhotos.net

Burmese Position

Image courtesy of adamr at FreeDigitalPhotos.net

This is the simplest position and is great for beginners.

- The legs should be crossed and you should be sitting on your zafu.
- Now, allow your feet to rest flat on the floor with the knees resting on the floor, too. The tops of your feet should be on the floor, not the bottom. Basically, you'll look like you're tucking your legs beneath you in the front.
- It can take a little bit of stretching in order for your knees to touch the floor, so don't be discouraged if you have to wait a few minutes or you have to practice a few times in order to get that far.
- If you need some encouragement for your knees, simply shift forward onto the first third of your zafu and sit straight. Now imagine that the top of your head is pushing toward the ceiling and stretch your body to get

your spine straight. Then let the muscles relax and go soft.

Half Lotus Position

Image courtesy of meepoohfoto at FreeDigitalPhotos.net

If you're going to use this position, get into the habit of alternating legs each time you meditate in order to keep the blood flowing properly.

- Sit down on your zafu and sit cross-legged.
- Now bring the top of your right foot on the top of your left thigh.
- Tuck your left foot underneath your right thigh.
- The position is somewhat asymmetrical and that is why you will have to alternate which leg you bring up each time.
- Your body should adjust to the differences and your spine should be straight.

You should look something like this:

Full Lotus Position

Image courtesy of stockimages at FreeDigitalPhotos.net

The full lotus position is the most stable of all the positions, but it can be the most difficult to perform.

- Sit on your zafu and cross your legs.
- Now, bring the top of your left foot up and place it on your right thigh.
- Bring the top of your right foot up and place it on your left thigh.

This position is completely symmetrical and the most stable of all the positions. However, it should be noted that the positions are not as important as what you are doing with your mind during this meditation practice.

Seiza Position

Image courtesy of Jonas Rabbe at Flickr.com

The seiza position can use just your body, a round, long pillow or a specialized bench known as the seiza bench.

- Put your knees on the floor and your feet behind you with the tops resting on your zafu.
- Now lower your buttocks until it's resting on our heels, your pillow, or your seiza bench.

This position will help you keep your spine straight and take the weight off your feet. It's a good position to use if you have any complications with your feet.

Chair Position

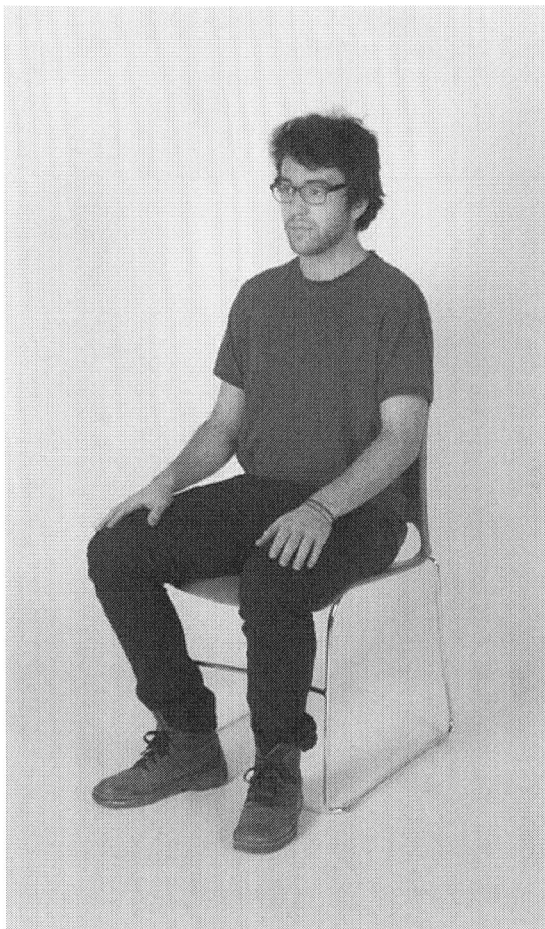

Image courtesy of Ananian at http://commons.wikimedia.org/

You may also sit in a chair if you do not want to put pressure on your legs. If you have any circulatory problems, sitting in a chair might be a better option. You can use your zafu under your behind on the chair or you can use it under your feet to make them more comfortable.

- Keep your feet flat on the floor.

- You can place your zafu underneath the feet, your behind, or between your back and the chair to keep the spine straight.

Tips Before you Begin

- You should keep your back straight and centered at all times because slouching will inhibit the diaphragm.
- Do not wear tight clothing, especially on the legs as this will inhibit circulation when you cross the legs.
- Do not control or manipulate your breathing. It will happen by itself, especially if you're in a comfortable position with good posture.
- Only breathe through your nose and keep your mouth closed unless you have a cold or another type of nasal passage blockage.
- The tongue should be pressed against the roof of your mouth. To do this, swallow once and then keep your tongue up in order to create a seal that will prevent you from swallowing or salivating.
- Keep your eyes lowered and your gaze resting on the ground in front of you.
- Your chin should be tucked in slightly.
- Keep tension out of your body.
- The upper torso should not be leaning either forward or backward and your nose should be in line with your navel.
- Your hands should be folded in the cosmic mudra. If you're right-handed, your right hand should be holding your left hand, both palms facing up. Your thumbs should be touching so that your hands form an oval shape. Your hands can rest on the upturned souls of your feet or on your thighs.

The Breath

Zen zazen focuses on the breath. It focuses on the area two inches above the navel, also known as the diaphragm. Your breaths should be effortless and easy rather than quick and fast. You will develop a deep relationship with your diaphragm or your hara.

Step One

To begin, start by rocking your body back and forth slowly in decreasing arcs until you're settled at the center of gravity. Your mind should be focused on the hara, your hands folded in the cosmic mudra, your mouth closed and tongue pressed on the upper palate, and you're breathing through your nose. Completely experience that breath and keep your attention on the hara.

Step Two

Begin to stabilize the mind by counting your breaths all the way up to ten. When you inhale and get to the end, that's one. When you exhale and get to the end, that's two. Do five sets of inhalations and exhalations until you reach ten.

Once you've reached ten, start back over at one.

If, at any point, you are interrupted by a thought and your mind continues to chase that thought, start back at one.

By counting your breaths, you are giving yourself feedback to help you understand when your mind has drifted away. When you return to your breathing, you are empowering yourself with the ability to think about what you *want* to think about rather than what your mind wants you to think about. This is known as the power of concentration or joriki.

Step Three

Once you've practiced this breathing exercise for a while, your awareness will becoming more prevalent and you'll notice things that were always there yet escaped your attention. The process of zazen is opening up your inner self and exposing it to what is currently happening around you.

Once you're able to count to ten and repeatedly get to the end without an effort to keep your thoughts from interfering, then you can star to count every cycle of breath. Each inhalation and exhalation will count as one.

So inhale, pause, exhale, and mentally say one. The next set it two, and so on and so forth. This will provide you with less feedback, but that is okay. This will get you to go longer without having wandering thoughts.

Step Four

Finally, you should be able to follow the breath without counting and just *be* the breath. Do not rush this part and do not expect to be able to get to this point the first time you sit down to meditate using this style. If you get to this point prematurely, you will not have a strong joriki, which will keep you from getting to Samadhi, a single-pointedness of mind.

Step Five

You should realize that random thoughts are going to pop into your mind at different intervals and that this is okay. Sometimes you may be involved in a crisis in your life and a thought seems to keep coming back. If you cannot get it to go away, allow that thought to run its course and then gently push it away. Zazen is not meant to suppress thoughts that need to be addressed, but rather to quiet the mind in order for us to focus on what needs to be focused upon.

Step Six

It will take you a long time to reach this point in zazen. Deep Samadhi or zazen is when a person breathes at a rate of only two or three breaths a minute. When we're normally at rest, we breathe fifteen breaths a minute. Your heart rate, circulation, and metabolism will all slow in deep zazen and the entire body will come to a point of stillness that you will not reach in deep sleep.

Be patient and persistent as you are practicing zazen, and stay away from thinking of any type of goal.

Shikantaza Meditation

You already know how to do this and probably have done it many times. You may have been hiking in the woods and came across a really nice view. Then you sat down and just looked at the view, and then something magical happened without you even realizing it. Your thoughts stopped and you just *were*. Or maybe you were listening to the bees or the birds going about their business on a summer day and your thoughts just ceased to happen as you felt one with the world.

Did you know that you can practice and cultivate this feeling?

It's best to start at home in a quiet setting in order to practice, but you can actually practice Shikantaza anywhere at any time.

Step One

Turn off the television, your cell phone, and any other electronic devices that may be a distraction. Then find a quiet place where you can sit. You do not have to be cross-legged or sitting on a cushion, sitting in a chair is just as well. Be sure to keep your back straight and your posture good.

Step Two

Place your hands on your thighs and close your eyes. Now feel your breath. Concentrate on those breaths and feel them entering your lungs and being released from them, too. Your mind is going to start showing you all kinds of thoughts and images as you do this, but allow them to drift away like a seed on a summer breeze. Do not try to stop them as they'll only get stronger, but allow them to float away.

Step Three

In Shikantaza, you will try to go even further than just letting the thoughts float away. You are going to try to enter a state of non-thinking. This will take a lot of time and practice, but you will eventually reach it. Don't worry about how much time you put in every day, even fifteen minutes is enough to get you started.

Step Four

Once you're finished, be sure to get up slowly and don't rush into your next task. Just let the relaxed feeling last a little longer before you return to your daily activities.

Even just practicing this a few minutes a day will allow you to put your mind on pause and refresh your thoughts.

Chapter Six – Mindfulness and Practices

As mentioned before, mindfulness is the most popular form of meditation in Western culture because it's simple and unique. Mindfulness teaches you to be comfortable with whom you are and teaches you to be unconditionally present as well as aware of what is happening in the moment. It is not about getting you to stop thinking, but rather to acknowledge those thoughts and follow them. Many people who are innovators and thinkers admit that they enter a state of mindfulness when they are attempting to solve a problem.

Mindfulness is paying nonjudgmental attention to the details of what we're experiencing as they arise and subside. You will not reject any thoughts or emotions as you are practicing mindfulness, and you should not be ashamed or embarrassed by any of them. Oftentimes, we experience an emotion such as happiness and worry that it will drift away, but mindfulness will allow us to hold onto that happiness for further use.

When you start to be mindful, you will feel that you are showing up for your life rather than missing it or being distracted by other things. Instead, if something has to be changed in our lives, we will be present enough to make that change. That is why a lot of people who suffer from stress, addictions, and mental disorders practice mindfulness.

Sitting Mindfulness Meditation

If you're just starting out with mindfulness meditation, sitting in a quiet area is probably the best way to begin. There are three parts to mindfulness meditations: body, breath, and thoughts.

Body

In order to relate to the body, you must first set up your environment. If you're using an eyes-open approach, you will want to have a set up a place within your home where you have a quiet place. It doesn't have to be an entire room, but just a corner of a room where you can sit and face that corner and see nothing but peaceful objects. You can create a small altar with pictures or photos from your own traditions or you can some candles or incenses as reminders of impermanence or just a plain wall.

Now you've picked your spot, you must choose your seat. You can sit on a cushion on the floor o in a chair. You can also use a folded up blanket or a low bench. The objective is to have a seat that is steady and comfortable, but will allow you to keep your back straight and your posture good.

Now that you have your seat sit down and be sure your posture is upright and loose. You don't want to be rigid. Your posture should remind you of someone who is dignified. The back should be straight with a curve in the lower back and your shoulders should be pulled apart gently. Keep your chin parallel to the floor and your arms at your sides.

When you are sitting on the floor, you should have your legs crossed and you should be comfortable. Be sure that your hips are higher than your knees, so add a pillow under your behind or a blanket. Your hands will rest on your thighs and face

44

down, and your eyes should be slightly open with your gaze on the floor in the front of you.

Now sit in this posture for a few minutes and bring your thoughts back to your body and your environment if they begin to wander.

Breath

The second part of this practice is the breath. You must rest your attention *lightly* on the breath. Just feel it coming in and out of your body and don't count or try to control your breaths. They should be coming in and out naturally. Don't think about whether or not your breaths are natural because this will lead to you controlling them. Just allow them to flow in and out at your natural rhythm.

Sit for a few minutes in the same position as you breathe in and out. Allow your mind to pay attention to your breath and acknowledge it, and then let it wander to your environment as well as your body.

Thoughts

The final thought and the main difference between mindfulness and other techniques is how you deal with your thoughts. In mindfulness, thoughts will arise and there may be a great many of them. You may experience memories, think about plans for the future, fantasies, and even what you saw on television. You may feel that there are no gaps at all where you can just focus on your breathing, but don't worry about this.

If you notice that you've gotten so caught up in your thoughts that you've forgotten where you're at and what you're doing, gently bring yourself back without any reprimands or judgment. You can tell yourself that 'thinking has just occurred' as if you're listening to the weather report.

If you're new to this practice, you should practice for ten to fifteen minutes and gradually increase those times to twenty or thirty minutes. You may extend this to forty-five minutes or an hour if you're experienced. If you're doing more than forty-five minutes, you may want to break up sitting meditation with walking meditation.

As a final note, remember that mindfulness meditation is not about getting yourself to stop thinking or be blank. It's about being with your thoughts and knowing who you are as a person and getting comfortable with that.

Walking Mindfulness Meditation

"When you look at the sun during your walking meditation, the mindfulness of the body helps you to see that the sun is in you; without the sun there is no life at all and suddenly you get in touch with the sun in a different way."

~ Thich Nhat Hanh

Image courtesy of Charisma at FreeDigitalPhotos.net

Walking meditation can be done while you're walking your dog, hiking, getting the mail or any other activity that involves walking. You should focus your mind one only one item such as the sound of the crickets or birds around you, or the feel of the ground underneath your feet, or even the color of the trees. When your mind begins to wander, catch it and return it to the original focus.

Red Light Meditation

Sometimes we have occupations that require us to spend a lot of time in the vehicle, and this is a good time to do some meditation techniques, but not while actively driving. Simply begin to practice taking deep breaths every time you get to a red light. When your mind wanders, bring it back to your breathing and the present.

Running or Cycling Meditation

Image courtesy of khunaspix at FreeDigitalPhotos.net

Focus on one sensation as you're running such as the sound or feel of your feet hitting the ground. Do the same with your cycling, such as the feel of the bike pedals beneath your feet or the feel of the sun on your face or neck as you're riding. Choose one thing to focus on and maintain that focus.

Eating or Drinking Meditation

"If you truly get in touch with a piece of carrot, you get in touch with the soil, the rain, the sunshine. You get in touch with Mother Earth and eating in such a way, you feel in touch with true life, your roots, and that is meditation. If we chew every morsel of our food in that way we become grateful and when you are grateful, you are happy."

~ Thich Nhat Hanh

This is particularly helpful if you have an eating disorder where you tend to overeat. This will help you slow down and savor your food rather than piling it in just for an emotional release. Focus on the flavors, textures, and sensation of the food as you chew it or drink it. Savor the feel of it and the taste while you take another bite. Be mindful of what you're eating.

Waiting Meditation

The next time you find yourself waiting in line at the supermarket or at the doctor's office, notice if your muscles are tense and whether or not you're hot or cold. Notice these differences in your body without judgment, and then expand your observations to what people have in their carts or what they're reading. Don't judge what they have, but rather just observe and notice without an opinion.

Task-Related Meditation

Focusing on what you're doing at the moment is a form of meditation that helps us pull ourselves out of our rivers of thoughts and focus on what's happening around us. So the next time you wash your hands, brush your teeth, fold your laundry, or take a shower, observe how you're feeling in that moment and what you're doing without judgment. Simply *be*.

Chapter Seven - Guided Meditation and Practices

Guided meditation involves all of the different meditation techniques. It is a live or recorded session where a person guides you with their voice, step-by-step, through a meditation experience. There are numerous different approaches to this, but all of them involve someone teaching you how to get where you want to be.

Some guided meditations have specific goals such as healing, self-improvement, and prosperity, improving relationships, forgiveness or stress-relief. Some are more general and aim to quiet the mind and produce relaxation and a feeling of calmness and peace. Some meditations, such as chakra meditations, are meant to bring about a higher state of consciousness.

Guided meditation can use imagery, which is describing a specific image to produce a type of experience or invite the listener to allow their imagination to expand. Others can be body-focused such as progressive relaxation or using breaths as a form of focus.

These types of meditations will inadvertently show the background and orientation of the guide as they are invariably influenced by their personal experience with meditation. Therefore, you should choose an instructor that has the same belief patterns as you.

People who both perform meditation regularly and who are new at the practice will benefit from guided meditation as it can bring about an entirely different viewpoint on the practice.

If you would like to find some audio on guided meditation, try this website: http://www.chopra.com/ccl/guided-meditations

Chapter Eight – Mixed Meditation Practices

Most meditation practices are actually a mix of two different of the four main types or more. You might be asking yourself why that is. It's because meditation is a mental balancing act and by having more than one technique, you're strengthening and widening that tightrope so it's easier to perform. A commonly used meditation technique that involves two different practices is Vipassana.

Vipassana

This meditation technique mixes two different forms of meditation: mindfulness and concentration. This seems like an oxymoron considering mindfulness is all about what is going on around you while concentration is about focusing on one thing, but you'll see what I mean in a few seconds.

Concentration and mindfulness are very different functions, but they each have a role in meditation and the relationship between the two of them in Vipassana is delicate and definite. Concentration is known as one-pointedness of the mind because it is forcing the mind to remain on one static point. It's a *forced* type of activity. It can be developed by sheer willpower and once develop, it still has some of that forced aftertaste.

On the other hand, mindfulness is a delicate function that leads to refine sensibilities. Mindfulness is the sensitive side that notices things going on. Concentration is the powerful side that keeps the attention pinned to one item. Mindfulness is in this relationship of concentration because you should be picking objects with mindfulness and concentration helps you keep them in sight.

In Vipassana, if either one of these forms of meditation is weak, you will have an imbalance and meditation will become difficult.

Concentration can also be described as a state of mind that focuses single-mindedly on an object without interruption, but true concentration is of a wholesome mindset. The state is free of hatred, delusion and greed. It focuses on the positive rather than the negative. If you focus on something negative while you are meditating, you will not have much help from the mind.

I'm going to go ahead now and tell you a form of Vipassana meditation known as body scan meditation. Know that there are many sub-meditations beneath Vipassana, but this is the one for beginners.

Body Scan Vipassana

Image courtesy of Asher Isbrucker at Flickr.com

Sit cross-legged in a chair or in another position that is comfortable. If you're not afraid you're going to fall asleep, you can even lie down for this one. Remember to keep your spine straight, so if you must put a small pillow or blanket beneath your lower back while you're lying down, go ahead and do so.

- Start with the top of your head or the crown area and observe the sensations there for a few seconds. Imagine that your mind is a scanner that is recording all of the sensations of an area but it doesn't have any internal comments for you.
- Now, continue to scan the face and back of your head for another five seconds.
- Do the neck area.
- Scan down to the right shoulder, your forearm and hand. Then go in reverse order back up your arm.
- Start with the left shoulder, go down to the forearm, and finally down to the hand. Now come back up in a reverse order again.
- Scan the front torso area and then the back torso.
- Scan the pelvic region.
- Scan your right thigh, leg and then foot and back in reverse.
- Scan the left thigh, leg and then foot and back in reverse.
- Scan upwards to the pelvic region, front, and back torso.
- Scan from the right hand up to the forearm and then the shoulder. Now do the left.
- Scan your neck, front and back.
- Now continue to scan your face and the back of your head.

- Finish up with the top of your head or the crown area.

Body Tense Vipassana

Image courtesy of apar yoga at Flickr.com

This form of Vipassana is just like the body scan form except you're actually tensing and relaxing your muscles. You should be lying down for this practice.

- Start with the right foot. Tense the muscles in your right foot and raise it off the floor about an inch. Then let it relax and drop.
- Tense your left foot and then raise it off the floor an inch. Now relax it and let it drop.
- Tense your right leg and raise it off the floor a few inches, then let it relax and drop.
- Tense your left leg and raise it off the floor a few inches, then let it relax and drop.
- Now tense your buttocks and your hips and raise it off the floor an inch, hold, and then let it relax and drop. You should begin to feel the blood flowing through your body and concentrate on that warmness or tingling.

- Lift your right arm off the ground a few inches and make a fist then let it relax and drop.
- Lift your left arm off the ground a few inches and make a fist, and then let it relax and drop.
- Pull your shoulders up to your ears and hold, then let relax them.
- Tense up your entire face and squeeze your eyes shut, and then let it relax.
- Move your head from side to side a few times slowly and gently, and then bring it back to the center.
- Now lie there for a few minutes and feel the energy permeating and flowing throughout your body.
- Lift up your arms above your head and stretch out your entire body, and then sit up and take a few moments to allow the blood to come back to your head.

This exercise is particularly good if you're suffering from muscle and joint aches and pains as it squeezes out the amino acids and other nutrients from your cartilage in your joints. This will help them heal quicker and bring down the swelling.

There are hundreds of different Vipassana techniques that originated from Buddhism, but these are the two easiest ones for beginners to practice.

Conclusion

Great amount of scientific research is there to show that health is better because transcendental meditation deals with consciousness, and consciousness is the basic value of all the physical expressions. The entire creation is the expression of consciousness.

~ Maharishi Mahesh Yogi

Meditation has come a long way from the prehistoric times when our ancestors sat and stared at the flames of their fires, but in a way, it's still the same concept. This practice is meant to bring about peace of mind and allow you to concentrate on the here and now rather than the past or the future. People who are experiencing stress, whether it's minor or extreme, report excellent progress in their mental state when they begin to practice meditation.

There's a reason this practice has been around for so long, and it will continue to thrive in this tumultuous world that we currently live in. Take the time to relax and allow your mind to be free of its worries for fifteen minutes a day and you'll begin to see why everyone raves about the benefits of meditation.

Remember that meditation is not religion specific and does not have to involve any belief in a higher lifeform. It's simply a state of mind that allows you to concentrate on your inner self and your thought process, as well as what is going on around you. There are plenty of people who do not believe in any religion who practice numerous different forms of meditation.

Also, don't forget to explore all the different types of meditation because you never know what might suit your fancy until you try it. Each mind is different and needs a different technique in order to flourish, so don't wall yourself off from meditation because you tried one technique and didn't like it. And have fun with it! Meditation is supposed to be about being light and free, not weighed down with specifics.

If you liked this eBook on Advanced Yoga Poses, please leave a positive review here. It will only take 1 minute but it is extremely important to me.

Thank you for reading!

With love and respect,

Robert Junior

Some Other Books From Us

Below you can find some of the other books published from us.

★Preview Start★

YOGA FOR
BEGINNERS

The Step By Step Guide Of Yoga Poses For
Beginners To Practice Meditation,
Manage Stress And Lose Weight

ROBERT JUNIOR

Yoga for Beginners

The Step By Step Guide Of Yoga Poses For Beginners To Practice Meditation, Manage Stress And Lose Weight

Preface

I want to thank you and congratulate you for downloading the book, **"Yoga For Beginners: The Step By Step Guide Of Yoga Poses For Beginners To Practice Meditation, Manage Stress And Lose Weight"**.

This book contains proven steps and strategies on how to learn the basics about yoga and through the practice of it learn the art of meditation, lower your stress levels, lose weight, become fitter and improve the overall level of your living conditions.

Throughout this book I am going to analyze in great detail many tips and tricks you can use in order not only to get in control of the whole thing but stay in control for the years to come.

As long as you follow the steps and guidelines you will read in this book I can guarantee you that you are going to see the first actual results and feel the difference within weeks.

This book will provide a lot of details on what is yoga, why is it important to practice it, how to be a yoga practitioner, in what aspects of your life you are going to see major improvement and how to stay on track in order to achieve your goals as fast as possible.

Thanks again for downloading this book, I hope you enjoy it!

Table Of Contents

Preface

Getting Started

The Origin Of Yoga

The Standard Format

Showing Up

Popular Types Of Yoga

Core Positions And Progression

Conclusion

Getting Started

The word 'Yoga' derives from the word 'yuj' in Sanskrit, meaning 'to unite.' This is appropriate given the multitude of purposes that yoga serves. Aside from the core reality that like-minded people from around the world come together quite often to share in its experience, yoga itself represents the unity of many different principles that can serve our everyday needs.

If you're reading this book you've already taken a step in the right direction. Yoga not only helps the practitioner get into better physical shape, it's a holistically beneficial activity. This book is going to help you approach yoga as a beginner and give you some tips to succeed in your quest for a better mind, spirit and body, which is what the practice of yoga is all about. Yoga's benefits are innumerable.

It's important to first dispel some of the myths about yoga. Despite being an activity that is sometimes associated with the feminine, there are many males that participate in the practice and there are a high number of male teachers. Some types of yoga, such as Hatha Flow, the most popular, are quite strenuous; enough so that it should instantly debunk any myths about yoga is too girly an activity for blustery males. Some also tend to believe that you need to be flexible to do yoga. This is patently untrue. Many yogis are not flexible at all, though the practice encourages them to expand their flexibility over time. Part of the rationale of yoga is accepting that bodies are unique and different. Respecting the limitations of your body is key and is also important in avoiding injury.

First let's discuss the body. Yoga has rejuvenating effects that surprise even veterans. A standard class lasts one and a half hours, and classes are often very strenuous. Yet at the end of them, yogis do not feel emptied of energy but just the opposite. Rather, they quite often feel energetic and ready for their day. Yoga classes are typically held throughout the day, running from as early as 5am to 7pm at night. Exercises are also extremely balanced, meaning that they practically focus on the body as a whole, rather than just one small part. In this book, students of yoga are referred to as 'yogis.' Experienced employees leading the class are simply called 'teachers' or 'yoga teachers.'

Avoiding Injury

Yoga is a very safe activity, as the entire practice typically takes place on a solitary mat. However an in any physical endeavor, especially involving strenuous exercise, there is a risk of overdoing things and injuring yourself. Here are a few ways not to do that. First, yoga should generally be avoided by women in the late stages of pregnancy. Generally at this point many of the poses are difficult to begin with. Also if there are prior injuries it's possible to exacerbate them. Yoga places a lot of pressure on the feet and the wrists. It isolates different parts of the body generally, and focuses on them one by one. Yogis with prior injuries in these areas could make things worse. Generally in the beginning of the class instructors will ask their students if they have prior injuries. It's important to be honest with them. If you ever need to take a break, particularly if in the course of the practice you are putting pressure on an area that makes you physically uncomfortable, there is nothing wrong with taking a break and going into the child's pose. You can wait there until the focus shifts to another body part. Some of the more challenging poses can be worrisome if the yogi does not have control. Beginners should be careful for instance when they try head stands and shoulder stands in the first few months of their practice. Generally a spotter is required to prevent balance from being lost, which could end up causing a cascade of teetering yogis, knocking each other over like dominos across the room.

Yoga etiquette

It's important to maintain yoga etiquette if you're going to a public class. It's not as if you'll be inundated by tons of different rules, but there are a few basic expectations that it's important to be aware of. The first of these is that you generally want to be early to class, so you have time to set up your mat (or a borrowed one) and get into a relaxed state. Class members sometimes chat when they first arrive, but as it becomes time to begin they are generally expected to fall silent and become attentive to the instructor. Bathroom breaks are fine, but are not all that common. The sessions are rather long (1.5 hours) so it's permissible to leave, but if you do just make sure not to disrupt the class. Some yoga centers may ask that males not take their shirts off during practice or that yogis avoid showing up already emanating unpleasant odors. This may seem strange given that yoga is a highly physical activity, but it's also meant to appeal to the other senses, including smell. There is generally incense burning in the room, so as to make for a pleasant aroma.

★Preview End★

If you liked the preview you can download a copy of the book here: http://amzn.to/1y5lwWo

Free Book

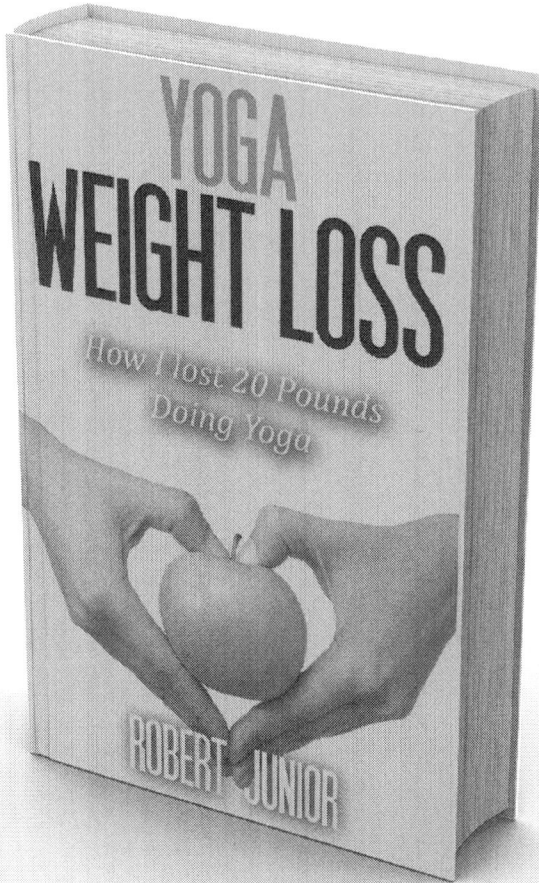

As a Thank you gift for downloading my book, I will give you my new book "Yoga for Weight Loss" for free.

Please follow the link here http://bit.ly/19eWRoW to download your free copy of my book "Yoga for Weight Loss" normally sold on Amazon for 2.99$

Thank You

16006251R00041

Printed in Great Britain
by Amazon